Dedication…

> *To my wonderful wife, Nancy, who has, for all of*
> *these years, put up with my bullshit: my bad*
> *jokes, mood swings, general pot stirring*
> *behaviors and basic "pain-in-the-assness".*

> *I love ya with all that I am!*

Table of Contents

A Cautionary Tale

If you have

- *"read me"* before or…
- listened to my internet-based radio shows (podcasts) or…
- watched my videos or…
- attended one of my live seminars or workshops…

then you are *aware of* and have *insight into* the fact that I am an intense, at times irreverent, energetic and passionate

Frequent Flyer to Hell <u>and</u> Back

For some of my most infamous trips to Hell and Back-of which you will read-I was dragged kicking and screaming, ranting and raving all of the way to the gates of Hell. I was an unwilling participant on those horrid journeys down the highway to Hell that resembled actually being in a *Mad Max* movie, while taking massive amounts of mind altering drugs and never being given a weapon to defend yourself.

I didn't want to go!

I didn't intentionally or even accidently book passage on the '63 Greyhound bus that tore down the road to the gates of hell.

I was taken, against my will, for a ride.

My life stolen.

My life ruined.

And for some of those trips, I actually **flew the plane** myself. I piloted my own plane, alongside of my co-pilot, "*Fred*", a one-eyed mule, straight to the gates of hell.

My hair on fire, smoking cigarettes, drinking beers, and wearing only orange underpants.

To the sounds of John Mellencamp, REO Speedwagon and others, I rocked that rainbow-painted DC-3 straight to Hell and enjoyed every frickin' minute of the journey.

Once at the gates of Hell, be it that you flew the plane yourself or are an unwilling passenger on that '63 bus, the only question left to answer is…

Do <u>YOU</u> Setup Camp?

Do <u>YOU</u> Stay at the Gates of Hell?

Or do you…get up, flip off Hell's most famous resident and walk away to find the highway of healing while shouting, "I'm outta of this frinckin' Hell hole."

When I pondered (and I am sure I will ponder this question again at some point in my life), those questions, I considered these facts: If I stay, if I choose to accept my fate and don't set out for the finding the highway of healing then I **<u>MUST</u>** also accept the outcomes of my decisions!

I **<u>MUST</u>** fully embrace the asshole I will become.

I **<u>MUST</u>** fully accept that my sobriety from drugs and alcohol will be challenged. And challenged mightily. If I go back to "*those days*" I **<u>MUST</u>** accept that I AM CHOOSING to drink and drug and CAN NOT blame bad-luck, life circumstances, anyone or anything OTHER THAN ME.

In all honestly, not wanting to bear the heavy burden of the personal responsibility of actually choosing to stay at the gates of Hell then watch my life drip into a sinkhole I chose healing. In some ways, my lack having my very own set of big balls, which are needed in order for me to say "fuck it" and allow my life to disintegrate in my hands, drove my choice to find healing.

It wasn't nobel.

It wasn't cool.

It wasn't "the right thing to do."

It was cowardice. I was too fearful of the outcomes of openly choosing to let my life go down the toilet.

So, I got my ass off of the ground and walked away.

I was not staying. I didn't have the stomach for it.

I would later learn that I may have wimped out related to "going all in" on allowing my life, and the lives of those connected to me, go down the drain. Avoiding this incredibly self-indulgent, ultimately selfish choice was far more brave and adventurous than I gave credit.

Staying is the easy choice.

Staying is the safe play.

Staying is what wimps choose.

I may have gotten up and moved away from the gates of hell out of fear of bearing the full weight of the personal responsibility for what my choice to sat may do to others; however, choosing to heal meant that I would endure incredible pain and panic and that accepting that road was far more courageous.

As you may have already determined my writing style is rooted in the **art of catharsis**:

a purging of pent-up and socially unacceptable cognitive and emotive tensions through artistic expression.

That means people, that my writing, radio shows and live stage presentations are roller coaster rides through my mind and soul and feature commentary denouncing __my__ human folly of vice-driven behaviors leveraged and rolled-out all in the name and good faith of healing. You have just signed up for a cathartic mayhem of stream of conscious rants and raves about life, love, loss, sex, family, music, movies & hockey AND HEALING!

I expose and comically explore the manner in which I interpret the world.

I lampoon and parody the psychological and theological status quo which directly impacts the manner in which I interpret the world and thus directly effects my healing plan.

I boldly encourage myself, and thus others vicariously through my artistic expressions, get my head out of my ass and my ass off of the couch. So, I encourage you to get your head out of your ass and get your ass off of the couch.

Why?

To heal!

And live a life desired and not only dreamed.

Come on people!

Live mentally well.

Enjoy the ride. Laugh often.

This Little Book WILL NOT BE:

Easy since healing is hard work and often something that is accidently on purpose avoided by most intelligent people who fear difficult times and pain. We talk ourselves out of the healing and grieving process because it is painful. It is much easier to avoid the pain and engage in ineffective and unhealthy healing attempts such as drinking, drugging, anger, isolation and many other behaviors. Not only is it easier, it is sometimes much more fun and satisfying. It is the fun and satisfying aspect that becomes the reinforcing agent that perpetuates these unhealthy and ineffective healing behaviors.

At the end of the day though, you can't bullshit yourself. You may think that you can; you can't. You can bullshit your spouse, kids, friends, family, boss, co-workers and people who ride the bus with you in the morning. You cannot bullshit yourself. You **KNOW** when the behaviors of which you are using to heal are not working.

Healing, Grieving and Changing are not easy. Let's just accept that now so that we can move on to the real work.

This little book is **NOT** *"Treatment"*. I am **NOT YOUR** therapist! I am a Licensed Clinical Professional Counselor. I received a Master of Arts in Counseling Psychology. I am writing as a griever who has been there and done that. So, I have the street and education "cred" to write a book like this, make suggestions and encourage you to heal. That does not make me or this book you pseudo counselor.

If at any time while reading this book you think or have the notion or feeling for one fleeting moment that professional support is what you need and want, then get your ass off of the couch and get a therapist. Don't think, ponder or debate with yourself. Visit www.counseling.org to locate a qualified professional in your area.

Oh, and screen and interview your counselor. Make sure the person you select can actually help you. Make sure that his/her methodology "fits" what you are looking for.

Counselors, like doctors, need to be selected carefully.

It's your mind and soul that is being healed, take ownership and make sure you find the correct healer for you.

This little book is **NOT** *boring* since I make grief and healing fun and entertaining.

This little book is **NOT** *a place to hide* since this book is going to trigger thoughts, emotions, physical sensations and behaviors in you that you may be uncomfortable experiencing. As you read you will find yourself thinking about significant events in your life that you may have buried away and forgotten. It takes a mere split second for a memory and/or imaginary fear to be recalled from the depths of your deepest and darkest places in your soul.

You are going to experience the *"snow globe effect."* Things become cloudy, out of focus then a new image appears.

I am going to poke you in your soul and challenge the manner in which you take in the world.

Well, here we go!

Guzzle those fuzzy lifting drinks. We are headed into the danger zone.

Start Your Engines

Ready to get started?

Healing is like NASCAR.

It is fast paced, exciting, dangerous and loaded with thrills and challenges. So buckle up, because when you grieve and heal accurately, you are in for the ride and experience of your life.

What is Healing?

Healing is the **natural process** by which we **triage the trauma** that is ushered into our life as a result of a life storm or crisis event.

In my books, workshops and seminars and even on my radio show I discuss healing in a linear fashion. Meaning that I describe (1) life events that rock our world, (2) the trauma those life storms create and (3) how healing helps us rebuild, reboot and reinvent ourselves and lives.

Books, workshops, seminars, videos and even the podcasts are linear: a point to point straight line discussion. Hence the limitation of media when it comes to exploring the vital and life giving-back *process* of healing.

Life is *process*. Life ebbs and flows. Life moves forward then backwards then sideways and even diagonally. Life is up then down then up again and down once more. Sometimes the up are high and the downs very low. Somethings the ups are just up and the downs just downs, nothing dramatic.

With this in mind I take a linear look at *why we heal* and *how we heal*. I call all of this *The Art of Healing*. You may choose to apply what you learn from reading this book by engaging in the process of living your life, the process of the Art of Healing.

Life Storms happen.

Crises occur.

Our lives rocked.

The trajectory on which we thought our life was traveling is suddenly altered. Sometimes subtly and sometimes violently.

Each and every day we are confronted with the events and situations that create the scenes of our life. These life events, some of which grow into life storms, impact our lives. We are also expected to cope with situational life events from hitting every light on the way to work and thus being late for the big meeting to the fact that no one in your home saved you a plate of dinner and post that late meeting you arrive home with the kitchen cleaned and dark and the family on the couch watching DVR fodder.

The other choice is to not cope, not manage the situational life events that challenge our mental wellness and psychological fitness skills. You can always dig a hole, crawl in and stop living so that you stop experiencing daily occurrences that challenge your mental wellness. Go on. Yell at the family for sitting on their collective asses watching television as you are forced to microwave a pasta bowl because no one had the forethought to save you a plate.

How rude.

No one loves me.

No one cares that I am out slaving away late into the evening.

Shit. Spilled pasta sauce on my new tie.

Life storms, which are known as "crises", break connections we have with vital people, places and things in our lives. When a divorce occurs, the connection between husband and wife; parent and child are broken. A connection to a dream of a happy and content family, awesome and loving marriage, romantic get-a-ways is broken. The connection to trust and faith and honesty is broken. Life storms break the connections we build and maintain that make life not only possible but rich and full.

Life storms also come with plenty of debris. As with a tsunami or tornado or hurricane debris and destruction are side effects of the life storms or crises in which we endure. Life storms leave behind the debris of fear and hurt.

When we lose our job we have a broken connection to coworkers and identity and a sense of productivity. We also see piles of debris: fear and hurt. We are afraid that we may never find another job like that ONE. God, how we loved that job. What a great team of people.

We may fear that we may lose our home due to a lack of financial income. Now what? Small one bedroom apartment for the five of us. Ok. We'll put the kids in the bed room. We have cots and sleeping bags. My partner and I will sleep on the sofa sleeper we'll pull out of some garage sale. Beats a refrigerator box under the highway bridge.

We may be hurt that after 25 years of dedicated service we were dismissed in a thirty-minute meeting with human resources then handed a small, paper box in which to pack up 25 years of history. And Gladys from HR. Crap. We had her and her husband on the boat last summer. BBQing burgers, fishing, tubing. And wow. No emotion. No heads up. Shit.

When a life storm enters our lives, thinking about all of the broken connections, new connections that need to be made, and the process of reconnecting, rebooting and rebuilding, trigger emotional responses (that debris of hurt and fear) as well as physiological sensations.

The emotive response (hurt and fear) and the physical sensations are TRAUMA.

Trauma is triggered when our mind and imagination interpreting the facts that our brain is collecting.

When you stand at the bedside of your child who battled leukemia so bravely for five years and your brain begins to realize that "this is the end" and your mind assembles those facts into a clear picture that your child will soon die, your soul and body respond.

Trauma is the real time, in the moment, right here and right now emotional and physiological response we experience when our mind interprets the world around us.

Trauma is ALSO the immediate, in the moment emotional and physiological response we experience when our mind memory recalls and paints a vivid past life experience.

Trauma is ALSO the immediate, in the moment emotional and physiological response we experience when our mind imagines the "future", a future scene that may never playout.

Most people enter counseling, go to their church, turn to drinking and/or drugging, become angry, become on isolated spending days on end in their underwear in the basement of their home watching Netflix and playing Xbox while eating Cheetos. Only to come above ground days letter looking like an Oompa Loompa.

Some of us, me included from time to time, attempt to triage trauma felt in the moment. There are times when I recall the death of my children. Kyle died in 1996 and Dakota in 2002. Yet, when my mind plays those dusty newsreels or my imagination creates a sequel feature of what could have been, what SHOULD have been emotions and physical sensations launch immediately when the memory or imagination play in the drive-in theater of my mind.

Those emotions are deep, dark, powerful and completely unwanted. The physical sensations are my brain's attempt to protect the body by launching the fight, flight, freeze response and taking my defenses to defcon 5.

Those toxic and boiling emotions and physical sensations designed to help me run my ass off to move away from danger or to kick the shit out of something in response to being threatened, must go somewhere. And if I cannot run or fight, those emotions and physical sensations build and build and build until all hell breaks loos and the fit hits the shan.

Those who effectively and in a healthy way triage their trauma do so through the development a set of psychological fitness skills that ultimately lead to a happy healthy life.

Those who don't continue to suffer with trauma.

Healing is, by its very nature, a natural attempt to triage the trauma we feel in the moment so that we may heal what our wounds and manage what frightens us so that we may live a happy healthy life.

Trauma is a waving, warning flag, flashing signal, bullhorn and huge neon sign that screams "healing" that tells us each and every day we need to heal. Miss the signals and stroll head on into a train or on-coming traffic.

To avoid being crushed by an on-coming train or traffic, we must learn how to triage trauma in the moment was it is experienced. Thus, we need to develop a set of psychological fitness skills that become the manner in how we manage the fear that we experience and heal the wounds that cause us pain.

We must also develop our own and customized unique healing and grieving plan. No two grieving and healing plans are the same. All of us are uniquely crafted and uniquely made. We all have a unique personality and temperament as well as a one of a kind life story. Thus we must work hard and persevere so that we may overcome adversity by building our own unique healing and grieving plan.

What is Crisis?

A crisis is a *life storm* or *life event*.

As we live our lives, we experience a variety of life events and storms. Some of these events, such as a:

- divorce,
- death of a loved one,
- lay-off,
- illness and/or
- foreclosure

are significant while others barely make our radar such as: missing the 3rd light on the way to work and thus delaying our travels by a whopping 2 minutes.

That's ok, though, because I have *Marauder Radio* on my iPod and I have a few minutes left in this eye-popping and soul-opening episode.

This book focuses on

- the significant life storms and events. And
- the significance of a storm or event is defined by **YOU**!

Not me or your spouse or children, parents, friends, pastor or even counselor. Oh no, you, and only you, have the responsibility of designating which life events and storms are significant or "blips on the radar." Taking responsibility for your healing starts now.

The life storms that you designate as significant are similar to natural storms such as tornadoes, hurricanes and tsunamis. Life and natural storms share two key elements in common.

First, life and natural storms break things.

Second, both leave behind a ton of debris.

Natural storms put cars in trees and boats in living rooms. Natural storms leave behind torn roofs, broken tree limbs, mangled lumber and drywall and tile and carpet that at one time were the components of someone's home. Now, those discarded components create a pile of garbage in the middle of a flooded community.

On November 17, 2013, a major, late fall storm hit the Chicago area. One of the many mighty oaks in my yard decided to ride out the storm in my home. For once in my life, I actually experienced the natural storm debris field (*as I described in seminars, workshops, books and on my radio show for years*) in my own home and life. What an ironic and iconic experience.

See appendix A for some of the pictures.

Life storms break our dreams, hope, faith, marriages, family and security among other things. Life storms leave behind debris piles I label: hurt and fear.

There are two categories of crises or life storms:

- On or Off Time Crisis and
- Situational Crisis.

An On or Off Time crisis is a life storm that is connected to a time-line. The time-line is often created by society, our family and/or us. Along with the time-line are a unique set of expectations held as *"beliefs"* by the community, our family, us or a combination of us and our family or community.

As an example, in the 1960's the time-line, meaning chorological age, for marriage was pegged at twenty or shortly after high school. Today that age has increased to twenty-seven. As we grew as a society and individuals, completion of college and one's initial career launch were "added" to the time-line and expectation list thus bumping marriage back a few years to accommodate for the new goals needing to be accomplished.

Following suit, most people start a family in their early thirties or late twenties. If you are forty and not married, you may experience a life storm due to the fact that you are "off schedule" with the life event of getting married and starting your family.

God help you if you are unemployed or under-employed as well since that would be three strikes. And you know what three strikes means: _____

(fill in your own answer here)

Time lines are flexible and are altered as societal values ebb and flow. For decades most people married and started their families in their early twenties. Today a twenty-something is not overly worried or sad if they have not married yet. Forty years ago someone of the same age might have felt pressure and even marginalized if they had not "settled down" by their twenty-eighth birthday.

Today, when you meet a couple in their mid-thirties who are without children the natural reaction is to wonder "Why?" Then our minds start to create a host of scenarios from infertility to choice. It appears "odd" to us when someone is off-time with society's time lines.

Situational crises are the direct effect of a sequence of events leading to a climaxing conclusion. Situational crises are the story lines of movies. The plot thickens and twists and turns until an ultimate breaking point is reached.

Situational crises can take weeks, months and even years to build or can be sudden, dramatic twists of fate.

The death of a loved one can be sudden, in the event of an accident, or the building and developing story line of an illness. One day you are playing golf and laughing with your friends and the next morning your doctors are discussing your treatment options for the cancer that was located during your last routing check-up.

Crises are a time of danger and incredible opportunity.

Crises are a time of danger since some of us choose healing behaviors that are ineffective and unhealthy. For a long time I dealt with the *Bullshit of Life* through addiction and anger. It was easier to drink and yell and drug and isolate than it was to face the pain, talk about, heal and then learn how to effectively manage the anxiety that came with having lost so much.

Those debris piles of hurt and fear that I discussed a few pages ago require clean-up. Learning our personalized and unique clean-up protocols is hard work and painful. The danger is that the hard work and pain deter us from working our way through to the other side where healing resides.

If we avoid the pain and hard work by taking the "easy way out" and use less than effective and healthy means of coping with the *Bullshit of Life*, then we can actually make the crisis event or life storm of which we are trying to cope even worse. We can spawn new storms and create new crises. If I turn to drinking to manage the anxiety and heal the hurt that I have after losing my job; I may also, due to my drinking, loose my marriage, connections with my children and friends.

Crises are also a tremendous moments of opportunity to learn who we are and the "stuff" of which we are made. Crises are times in which we develop character and perseverance. We forge our resiliency and develop skills that carry us past this life storm and event as well as through the life storms and events yet to occur in our lives.

We develop confidence in our own intuition and our ability to predict and anticipate the outcomes of our healing behaviors.

We learn that we will survive and be stronger.

Our relationships to people, places and things will grow deeper and more intense and become the bedrock on which we build our healing platform.

As Tim McGraw's *Live Like You Were Dying* ballad suggests, we "love deeper" and life is "sweeter" and we live more fully as human beings.

The Impact of a Crisis

Crises are life storms that rip through our lives with the same force and destructive elements of a tornado, hurricane and/or tsunami.

Life storms or crises break vital and life giving connections we have created with people, places and things during the course of our lives. Connections to people, places and things are the very fabric of our lives. Connections are how we get our needs for love, significance, belonging, fun and freedom as well as basic survival[i] met.

In order to live, experience the best that life has to offer and improve the quality of our lives moving forward, we must have connections to people, places and things. When a life storm or crises breaks a connection, healing is the art of rebuilding the broken connection.

Sometimes the connection cannot be mended, as in the death of a loved one or when we are the victim or offender of violence. We must build a new connection in order to get our needs met, heal and rebuild our life, faith, trust, hope and dreams.

For every life storm and crisis a variety of connections are broken. It is impossible to list all of the connections broken due to life storms since each one of us is unique and different. We may share similar tales of life storms such as death of a loved one, divorce, homelessness and/or illness yet the connections broken will vary due to our uniqueness and one of a kind life story.

When I buried my two children who died as a result of a congenital heart defect, my broken connections included those with faith, family, son, daughter, marriage, dreams and hopes. These connections were unique to me and offered me a personalized and customized means to get my needs met. Without the connections, I my needs go unmet. Although my wife and I suffered the exact same loss and traveled on the same flights to Hell and back; we each have different needs that were met through those connections. We need to rebuild existing connections and construct new ones in order to heal. Those connections will vary as our needs are unique to each of us.

Life storms, like natural storms, leave behind a ton of debris known as **hurt** and **fear**. Failure to *"clean up"* the hurt and fear can lead to unhealthy and ineffective expression of those emotions that lead to additional life storms.

When my children died, the pain of that loss was immense. Each and every day was a burden just to get up, shower and attempt to go about my daily life. Even today, years later, when I think of their deaths and the lost chance of raising them or I wonder what they would be like today, I feel immediate and soulful pain and my body responds as well in the form of tight shoulders, dry mouth, dizziness and sweaty hands.

I also feel tremendous anxiety as a result of Kyle and Dakota's deaths. I worry constantly about the safety of my living children. I make deals with God that since He already has two of my children he can't fucking having any more. I worry about the next great life storm and wonder: will I and can I take another setback or will that be the straw that leads to my own rapid downfall into a pit of despair from which I never arise.

The hurt and fear are REAL TIME emotive experiences I endure.

This is called Trauma, which I will discuss in more depth later in this little book.

There are many ways in which I can heal my hurt and manage my anxiety. I can choose healthy and effective behaviors to heal and manage. I can choose unhealthy and ineffective behaviors. I can also leverage, and thus choose, healthy and effective connections to people, places and things and thus get my healing and grieving needs met. I can choose unhealthy and ineffective connections. It's all about ME and MY choices.

At the end of the day, triaging my trauma and cleaning up the hurt and fear debris as well as mending and building connections is all in my control. As it is with you too.

That level of responsibility scares many people.

If the hard work, pain and guts that are required for genuine healing doesn't freak you out then the level of personal commitment may just do the trick.

Healing is not for wimps.

Understanding the Life Storm

Healing is:

Mending the connections that were damaged in the storm.

Mending broken and damaged connections means that we may need to offer and ask for the dreaded "F-Word":

forgiveness.

The trick with forgiveness is that if we expect someone who has hurt us to ask for forgiveness in order for us to clean up debris we have given control of our own healing to another.

That cannot happen.

That is not how healing works.

Our healing, grieving and happiness cannot and will never be dependent on the behaviors of anyone other than ourselves.

Sometimes, we need to ask for forgiveness. As a drunk and addict who has not had a drink and/or a drug today, when getting sober and healing my life, I engaged in a series of steps that required that I take a fearless moral inventory of my life and the damage I did to my life and the lives of others as a result of choose to drink and drug. Then, I had to offer amends, seek forgiveness WITHOUT expecting that from the people in my life that I disappointed, let down, hurt, destroyed. I hurt many.

If those whom I hurt HAD to grace me with forgiveness, I would not heal. The focus of these healing actions is for me to own and accept responsibility for my choices, actions and consequences that followed my choices. The goal is not absolution as if it is a suave for my own wounded soul, oh no! That is the opposite of accepting personal responsibility for the crap I did to others.

Healing is:

Move in ANY direction away from the storm.

People often say that they need to "move on."

I have said it.

I hate when others tell me I need to "move on."

It's OK for me to say it to myself and never OK for someone to say it to me. A little "rule of healing" I live by.

Thus, I never tell another to "move on." Instead I suggest that they just move up/down, left/right, forward/back or diagonal. I don't care. Just move in any direction away from the storm.

Healing is:

Building new connections.

Healing is a unique and personal process that is completed within a loving and supportive community. I may have a connection with my bicycle and the local bike path that winds through the state park. Although a solitary healing behavior, I have build connections to people (other riders or walkers to whom I nod or smile at), places (the park and that little tree I sit under by the pond) and things (my bike, nature and music stored on my MP3 player).

On the other hand, I may join a bowling league, make new friends, bowl at a new center I have never frequented and then share a meal with my team at a new watering hole. I have highly social and interactive connections with people (my team), places (the lanes and restaurant) and things (bowling, chicken wings and socializing).

Healing is:

The development of psychological fitness skills[ii] ©.

In order to figure out how to best heal the wounds of the past and manage the anxiety that plagues our lives we must try things out, evaluate their effectiveness and improve upon those skills **daily**.

Like I said, healing is not for wimps and is hard work.

What is Trauma

When it comes to the word "Trauma" there is plenty of confusion to go around. The word trauma can mean many things.

Trauma can mean that there is either a physical or emotional or even spiritual wound.

I can break my arm and be taken via ambulance to a **trauma** treatment center. Then describe to the medical team the dramatic moment of falling off of the roof while attempting to free my child's Happy Birthday Mylar balloons from my dish so that I can watch the end of the Daytona 500, which is why I missed her 4th birthday party in the first place.

I can walk in on my wife with the neighbor, two dogs a chicken and a one-eyed mule named "Fred" then tell the divorce lawyer that it was "**traumatic**.

I can say that my pastor's calling my pending divorce from my wife who loves a hooved audience as not "God's plan" and that "I need to forgive and invite her back into my world" as **devastating**.

In the world of counseling we have a diagnostic label of PTSD or Post Traumatic Stress Disorder. In my world there is nothing "post" about trauma. Trauma is real time!

In my workshops and books it is important to identify the nomenclature or theoretical structure to help the reader and the workshop attendee understand that of which that I am referring, a fairly straightforward process. However when we are out in the real world living our lives throwing words around can often be confusing and not very helpful. Therefore it is important for us to have of flexibility in our nomenclature as we lead our lives and attempt to heal. When you hear or in this case read the word **"trauma"** what comes to mind? Take a moment to think about that for yourself.

For the purpose of this book I'm going to define trauma in the following ways:

Trauma is *an automatic emotional response.*

The emotions that most of us experience when life storms enter our lives are either hurt or fear or both. These emotions cannot haunt us or pain us or fill our souls with darkness unless we start thinking about or pondering or imagining a crisis event. As I described in the earlier chapters of this book a crisis is a life event. When we attempt to make sense, understand, integrate and apply that life event into our lives we open the door for trauma.

Trauma is also *an automatic physiological response* that we experience when we attempt to understand a life event or crisis. In fact most of us recognize the physiological elements of trauma long before we notice the emotional ones. And even longer before we ever connect our emotive and physical response to the work of our brain recalling the facts and our mind assembling those facts into a film strip that contains *the movie of our life.*

Some of the things that we may experience physically when we experience trauma are tense muscles, increased heart rate and lung capacity, blood rushes to our extremities and we become flush, our stomach or head may begin to hurt and cortisol, a steroid hormone, is dumped into our brains in an effort to prepare our bodies to fight, flight or freeze. When we are threatened or wounded, we have an innate behavioral response to protect ourselves by kicking something's ass (fight) or running our ass as fast and as far as possible away from the threat (flight). When we are so overwhelmed, we do nothing, we freeze.

Anxiety can also drive confusion.

As it is with trauma the word "anxiety" is often confused by many people as well.

For me anxiety is an emotive response that is neither good nor bad; right nor wrong.

Anxiety is triggered by thought. Anxiety is what fuels certain behaviors. Anxiety is what many of us refer to as an emotive response. And that response has a continuum that spans mildly worried to unbelievable panic. Anxiety is also, as we have identified with trauma, accompanied by physiological responses which may include sweaty palms, dry mouth or shaking hands. For some the word "anxiety" is a mental health diagnosis that covers a series of emotional and behavioral criteria an individual needs to experience during a stressful situation.

Anxiety can and often is very beneficial as we manage our lives. If we didn't feel anxious we would drive to work at a 100 miles an hour not paying any attention to stop lights or pedestrians. Anxiety can help us be prepared. If you are anxious before a speech or a big test chances are you'll be more focused on the functional tasks of speaking or taking the test than you would be if you didn't feel any worry or concern. Anxiety can often spring us into action. If you're worried that you may lose your job you may start writing a resume or filling out job applications. The very act of writing your resume and completing job applications helps to reduce the emotive experience. Meaning that the best medication for anxiety is often action.

Therefore anxiety can be beneficial in that it helps motivate us to action.

It is when the anxiety becomes overwhelming and we are unable to be motivated or act in a functional manner that anxiety becomes a problem. As with speaking or test taking, if the anxiety is do high and you lack the skills necessary to cope with elevated emotions of fear, you may freeze and thus do poorly on the test or be booed right off of the stage.

Residing across the street from anxiety is depression. Depression, just as with anxiety, is triggered by thought. When we begin to evaluate and think about and contemplate and even ponder a crisis event we can start to feel "depressed". Depression is in emotive state that is neither good nor bad; right nor wrong. It too is a continuum of emotional experiences that range between just feeling "bla" to experiencing major "blues". Depression also is accompanied by physiological responses that may include muscle aches, sleepiness or fatigue, a lack of interest in food and of course head and stomach aches. Depression is a diagnosis, a label we assigned as someone who is experiencing a medical condition. Depression drives behavior.

Can depression ever be beneficial?

The answer is a resounding **YES**!

If I did something to someone the I start feeling "depressed" I may at some point ask the individual to forgive me. As it is with any word used to communicate a thought or concept "depressed" used in the last sentence could also mean "guilty".

The point is I feel bad.

If I'm sad that I missed a great hockey game because I forgot to set my DVR and I share that with my wife or my friends my expressing my "sadness" or "disappointment" or "frustration" is a good thing. I'm getting rid of my "sadness" or that pit in the bottom of my stomach as well as building intimate connections with my wife and friends.

I could go on for hours on how the notion of feeling sad or even afraid can be beneficial to us human beings learning how to heal and improve the quality of our lives. However, since I'm generally lazy and don't like such things, let's move on.

The primary reason for trauma, the primary reason we experience the emotions of hurt and fear, the primary reason we experience the physiological side effects, the primary reason we experience anxiety and/or depression is:

to tell us that we <u>require</u> healing!

Trauma indicates that we need healing. We need to heal and triage the anxiety or fear that prevents us from living our lives to the fullest. We need to heal and triage the depression that prevents us from connecting with important people, places and things in our lives that make our world enjoyable and rich. Often hurt and fear, if left unhealed, leads to the potentially destructive, ineffective and unhealthy behaviors of anger and addiction.

Trauma is a symptomatic episode that tell us **we need to heal**. Anger and addiction are symptomatic episodes that tell us **we need to heal**.

When we miss the signals of trauma, healing never starts. When we avoid or ignore the signals of trauma, healing is stunted or regressed. When we don't see the symptomatic signals of trauma our current connections to import and people, places and things can become compromised, weakened and in some cases broken and destroyed beyond all recognition. Dysfunctional behaviors, such as anger, addiction and isolation, are often used to mask the pain and panic that we experience. Trauma is the signal that healing is required. Dysfunction and emotional dysregulation are the signs that we have messed the symptomatic signals of trauma or simply have chosen to willfully not to engage in the healing process.

What is Grief?

As I have indicated often in this book, the words that we use to label "crisis" and "trauma" can confuse us, well me for sure, as we attempt to improve the quality of our lives and engage in a personalized healing plan.

That being said....There is no greater confusion in the world of healing then the mayhem swirling around the word **"grief"**.

Grief is not just *about the death* of someone whom we love. That is "grief's" primary role assigned by our society; however that is only half of the story, hell, that's only five percent of the story. Grief is so much more than how we respond to a death of someone whom we held dear. Yes, the death of a loved one is a "biggie" yet if we limit the natural healing process of grief to just death we'd never get better when it comes to healing from a divorce, loss of a job, and so on.

Grief is behavioral.

Grief is a natural healing process.

Grief is the whole ball of wax.

Grief is how we mend the broken connections to people, places and things that are so vital to a happy and healthy life.

Grief is how we triage trauma that plagues our lives.

Grief is healing!

Grief is Behavioral

When we grieve, we act through behaviors. We use behaviors designed to help us express our emotions as well as expel the physiological sensations our soul and body experience when we recall or imagine a life event.

As an example, when I think about the death of my children, my fills with hurt and fear. My body responds. I may cry. Crying is an automatic physiological response to my mind recalling the death of my children. My deep sadness is fueled by understanding that I will never be able to raise my beloved and wanted children.

Writing this book, becoming a counselor, facilitating a seminar on grief and producing my radio shows (podcasts) are all carefully selected grieving/healing behaviors in which I act in order to help me express my deep sadness and fear. As well as burn off some of that energy created by thinking.

I also express my happiness and joy for healing through writing, performing and speaking. As it is so true for some many things in life, healing is not just all sad and fear. Healing is also happiness. Healing is not all about crying, tense muscles and stomach and headaches. Healing is also about hugs, kisses, fist pumps, and dancing.

Grief is a Natural Healing Process.

Grief is how we respond to a loss, broken connection. In additional grief is how we respond to the emotional and physiological response our soul and body experience when we think about the broken connection, loss and the significance of such as loss.

Grief starts automatically. Just as your body heals when you scrape your knee, get the flu, or even break your foot, as I did a couple of summers ago. Even though I thought I had just pulled a muscle, I had actually broken my foot. Even without me going to the doctor, getting an x-ray, then wearing a boot (all things I should have done months before I actually did visit the doctor) my foot began to heal all on its own.

Healing starts whether you want it to or not. You naturally engage in behaviors that you believe will help you heal post a life storm or crisis or loss.

Perhaps you lost your job five minutes ago,

five days ago,

five weeks ago or even five months ago.

No matter. Thinking about *that* moment, in which you learned of your fate, creates trauma in your world *that* moment in which you think about the loss or crisis.

When we lose a job, connections are broken. The life storm dumps debris: fear and hurt. When in the right mind, after losing a job, wants to experience the pain and panic as we consider and think about the significance of the broken connections connected to the loss of a job? No one.

So, we start healing immediately. We grieve automatically.

Grieving is writing a resume.

Healing is applying for jobs.

Grieving is going on interviews.

Healing is networking.

Grief is a natural healing process. As you naturally and automatically develop your job search action plan, apply for positions, schedule interviews, network with colleagues, you generate options for your future employment which fosters faith in your skills and ability to secure a position. Faith produces hope which is the rocket fuel for motivation.

What if instead of reaching out, networking, applying for jobs, writing a resume, a person, who was suddenly unemployed, sat in the basement all day drinking or was unable to get out of bed or hid their unemployment from everyone by "going through the motions" of going to a factious job, are they healing? Are they grieving?

Absolutely.

The naturally and automatically sought out behaviors they thought would bring relief to the trauma experienced as a result of the job loss. Some may say that drinking and drugging all day or staying in bed or hiding the unemployment is NOT HEALING. Truth is, those behaviors are selected activities that someone who is unemployed thought would bring the most relief.

Those behaviors may not be as effective and/or healthy as say going to the library to network electronically or seek positions on a job website or go to a church support group to those recently separated from their employment. Yet who is to say?

In a nutshell, grieving is all about:

Identifying a specific and selected group of behaviors that
effectively and in a healthy ways
express emotions and
expel physiological responses.

Grief Style: You Got One

All of us have a unique grieving and healing style. It is through this one-of-a-kind style that express our emotive and physical response we experience as we think about and add meaning to the life storms we endure. Our grief style also helps us mend the broken connections to people, places and things that have resulted due to a life storm.

As an example, if I experience the life storm of infidelity in my relationship, my interpretation of the "**meaning**" of my partner's infidelity or the "**meaning**" of my own infidelity drives emotional and physiological responses. If my partner was unfaithful and I believe that "*I am victim*" my emotive response to my belief that I am a victim may be deep sadness. My physiological response may include a tensing of my muscles, shallow breathing, an increased heart rate, sweaty and shaking hands. If I do not find a healthy and effective set of behaviors to help me express my deep sadness as well as help expel the physiological sensations I may implode or explode, leading to even more issues.

Grieving behaviors help us mend as well as create new connections to people, places and things that are vital to our healing process. I may choose not to mend the broken relationship created because of my partner's infidelity. Or my partner may choose not to reconcile the relationship that my behaviors damaged. Regardless, I must develop behaviors that help me build new intimate connections with another partner. If I avoid my need for an intimate connection and fail to engage in behaviors that lead to me potentially meeting a new partner I may implode or explode. And that is definitely not good. Isolation is NOT a long term option for anyone.

Grieving behaviors help us learn how to manage our fear and soothe the hurt that arrive quickly when we are reminded of painful and frightening life storms. The infidelity in my relationship isn't the first and won't be the last time that I was/will be hurt by someone close to me.

It will happen again.

It is a part of life.

However after loving and living with an unfaithful partner, ending a relationship, and moving away from that pain and panic I am going to be hypersensitive to an intimate partner misleading me or possibly betraying my trust. Therefore when a current event triggers the memory of a past life storm, I must be able to emotionally regulate so that I don't implode or explode.

Healing is a shit load of work!

Grief, as a natural healing behavior, is a selected set of psychological fitness skills that we try, select, employ then modify over and over again. Our development of our unique set of psychological fitness skills, designed to help us heal from the trauma we experience as a result of a crisis, is really all about trial and error. When grieving, we try this healing behavior then we try that healing behavior. We see how this healing behavior and how that healing behavior pan out. If it works, it becomes a part of our unique psychological fitness skill set that helps us heal and improve the quality of our lives.

Some of the psychological fitness skills in which we engage are based upon our personality. As an example, I give workshops and produce a radio show. Both of these behaviors are incredibly healing for me as I am extroverted and highly expressive. My wife, who is more introverted and less expressive than I, prefers to volunteer and help others on a one-to-one, low keyed basis. Both of us have unique personalities and temperaments. Therefore what works for me may not work for her and vice versa.

So much of our psychological fitness skill set, which make up our healing and grieving behaviors, are unique to us; because we are unique people.

If you are introverted than most of the psychological fitness skills you engaging in will be relatively introspective.

On the other hand, if you are extroverted chances are many of the psychological fitness skills in which you will use to heal are associated with social or performance oriented behaviors.

Our life story is also critical to the development of our psychological fitness skill set.

Grief is incredibly difficult.

Grief is painful.

Grief is work.

And many times people avoid grief because of its difficultness and painfulness. This is normal and expected. No one can grieve 24/7. Occasionally we must stop our healing journey and rest. Remember though there is a world of difference between stopping for a moment to catch our breath and actively avoiding the grieving and healing process.

Grief can also be incredibly lonely. Because our healing process is so unique to who we are there are times when we may find ourselves isolated and alone because the psychological fitness skills that we need to heal are not the same skills that our friends or spouse or life partner need in their healing journey.

Grief is unique to each and every one of us.

There is no rule book.

There is no owner's manual. Well, that's not entirely true, since this book is a bit of a "manual."

There is no "how to" – again, not really true since this book is a bit of a "how to".

I guess what I am saying is that your play, your healing approach is uniquely developed by you with the assistance of this and other resources that get you thinking about YOU.

What YOU NEED to heal.

HOW you WANT to heal.

At the end of the day grief is a trial and error life experiment that requires full devotion and commitment.

How Grief Works

To understand grief as a healing process we need to really establish a model or a blueprint.

I know. This stuff is already heavy and now we need a "model." Wouldn't be a self-help and psychology book without a model.

We also need to understand the sequence or the assembly of this model. Understanding and having an appreciation for each component's contribution helps further our understanding of how the "system" works as a whole.

We begin to also appreciate the system and its complexity.

The beginning of the healing/grieving model suggested in this book is leveraged upon the work of Dr. Albert Ellis. Dr. Ellis was a cognitive behavioral psychologist who is credited with developing Rational Emotive-Behavioral Therapy or REBT. REBT features a simple model called: A-B-C.

In the A-B-C model **A** stands for "*action*".

Combining REBT's A-B-C model with my concepts already discussed in this book, the **A** or "*action*" is a crisis or life event. When you think of your own life, some of the "actions" or life events that you have experienced may include: the death of a loved one, the loss of a job, bankruptcy, emptied nesting, divorce, a medical diagnosis or being a victim of a crime. The list is exhaustive. The list is also unique to YOU and YOUR life story.

The **B** of the A-B-C model stands for "*belief*".

The belief is **YOUR** interpretation or attempt to understand the life event or "*action*". YOUR belief is the meaning that you apply to a specific life event or "*action*". The belief can sometimes be a logical or illogical; it may even be rational or irrational. At the end of the day the belief, the meaning that YOU attach to a crisis event. YOUR BELIEV is the very root of your trauma.

Getting to a belief the drives trauma is one of the toughest parts of healing. It is extremely painful to be mindful and aware of the beliefs that we hold and the interpretations that we create about the events of our lives.

When trying to get to a belief that drives trauma use this little device:

When I think about (*a life storm here*) it means that I'm:

_____

Fill in the rest of the Sentence Here

The **C** in the A-B-C model stands for "*consequence*".

A consequence is the automatic emotional response that we experience when our belief is triggered. That automatic emotional response may include hurt or fear or a combination of these two primary emotions.

In addition a consequence is an automatic physical response. We may cry or laugh, our muscles may tighten, we may experience a headache or stomachache, we may not be able to sleep or eat or perhaps we over sleep and over eat.

And finally a consequence is the healing behavior that we deliberately select to help us express the emotions of hurt and/or fear as well as expel the physiological responses we experience and fulfill our need for healing.

When the consequence is working for us, in other words when our behavioral choices are healthy and effective, we evaluate the consequence or the outcome of our behavior as "good". A healthy an effective consequence indicates that we are using healing behaviors in a way that we believe to be good. If our needs are being met the healing behaviors that express the emotions we feel and expel the physiological sensations we experience are healthy and effective. This is a good thing.

We are healing our trauma.

We are building new connections to people places and things.

We are mending broken connections.

When the consequence is not working, is ineffective or unhealthy, we evaluate the outcome of our selected healing behaviors as "bad". We realize that the healing behavior selected does not effectively eliminate the physiological sensations experienced when a belief is triggered. We evaluate and become insightful that the healing behavior selected does not express the emotions experienced in a healthy way. Our connections to people places and things are being damaged even more. We find that we are not healing; rather we are more destructive.

The Style of Grief

At one point in my now somewhat famous career some of the leadership team at a church grief support program asked me to speak on the differences between the manner in which men and women grieve. Like most folks I just bought into the myth that men and women grieve differently. The more I dug into the research and the more I looked into this specific tale I began to find that the manner in which you grieve has less to do with gender and much more to do with personality and temperament.

The work of Martin and Doka (1999) is of particular interest to me. Their published work resonates with my natural thinking and instincts on the *Art of Healing* and the *Art of Grieving*. Their work also just seems to make sense. These two researchers suggest that there are **two primary styles of grieving**: *intuitive* and *instrumental*.

The **intuitive** griever uses a series of healing behaviors that include open expression of emotion.

An Intuitive griever has very little problem crying when they're discussing the crisis event of their life.

An Intuitive griever has no problem with a public display of emotion.

An Intuitive griever is comfortable with loud and cathartic styles of communication.

An Intuitive griever openly expresses emotions through song or dance, writes music, poems, books, creates pieces of art and then proudly displays the work for all the world to see.

You can tell the moment you meet an intuitive griever how he/she is doing THAT DAY; heck THAT MINUTE. You won't have to ask them how they are feeling. Because they're going to tell you before you can even open up your mouth.

An Intuitive griever wears his/her emotions on their sleeves.

An Intuitive griever attends support groups.

An Intuitive griever heals by sharing what he/she is thinking.

An Intuitive griever heals by communicating with others.

An Intuitive griever heals by learning from and listening to others who are experiencing similar trauma or who have experienced a similar life storm.

An Intuitive griever also has zero problem going to counseling. In fact an Intuitive griever enjoys sitting down with a professional because they know that the professional counselor will assist them in further find tuning their already highly intuitive skills of healing.

An Intuitive griever heals by coming along side of others. An Intuitive griever after completing the support group may become the support group leader.

An Intuitive griever gives workshops and seminars, writes books and hosts a radio shows.

An Intuitive griever loves to teach other people about ways of healing.

An Instrumental griever on the other hand values solitary time. An Instrumental griever heals by going fishing or taking long walks. An instrumental griever will find incredible comfort in being on their own, by praying, by listening to music or simply reading a book. An instrumental griever loves solitary time.

There is a world of difference between solitary time and isolation. An instrumental griever may be perceived as isolating however an instrumental griever will be the first to tell you that their solitary time is vitally important to their own healing process.

An instrumental griever needs to know why the crisis event occurred or what series of events triggered the ultimate crisis event. An Instrumental griever heals by reading and researching and gaining knowledge about the very events that created their trauma. An Instrumental griever reads about the cancer or the illness that has changed their world.

An Instrumental griever gets tremendous satisfaction and takes great pride in his/her ability to control his/her emotions.

An Instrumental griever heals by problem solving.

An Instrumental griever heals by starting clubs or social groups or clauses that directly attack the topic or issue related to their crisis event.

An Instrumental griever heals by fixing.

An Instrumental griever takes it upon him/herself to keep up the gravesite or create a photo opal of their loved one or a video series.

Anger: a Grieving Train Wreck

Before I begin this chapter let's get out of the way a few presumptions.

1. You will get angry **again** before you die.
2. Anger is a human response and normal.
3. Anger can be diagnostic.
4. Anger can save your life.

So what exactly is anger?

Anger is the sound that hurt and fear make an as they leave our souls!

Anger is a behavior! Anger is **not** an emotion.

Anger, *as a behavior*, is the way in which each and every one of us expresses the hurt and fear trapped in our souls.

Anger, *as a behavior*, is the way we expel the physiological sensations experienced when our brain believes that we are in danger or about to be wounded.

Anger is a series of specifically selected behaviors that we choose to help us express toxic emotions, expel physiological sensations and get our needs met.

Although some of the anger behaviors, in which you engage, may appear to be *"automatic"* at one time YOU deliberately selected THAT specific anger behavior to express emotions, expel physiological sensations and ultimately get what YOU wanted. And it worked. So it became part of your behavioral arsenal for getting what it is you want.

Anger works.

Pure and simple.

Just like any other behavior if it gets us what we want, if it helps us expel the toxic pain and panic and get rid of the unwanted and elevated physiological sensations we continue to leverage THAT anger behaviors over and over again; regardless if it is effective and healthy.

Anger behaviors are triggered by how we think about our lives, our relationships as well as the past, present and future major events that make up that movie of our life.

Anger behaviors are fueled by the automatic emotions of hurt and fear and the automatic physiological sensations we experience, and I refer to as trauma in this book, that are triggered by us thinking about and attempting to a understand and apply meaning to the life storms or crises that plague our lives.

If we're really being honest with each other and you are being genuine with yourself and I am being authentic with myself we will agree that anger feels good! Anger works because it often gets us what we want: the expression of toxic emotions and the elimination of unwanted height and physical sensations.

Anger can be justified.

Anger is a choice.

Anger is learned.

Anger is reinforcing.

Anger can be internalized. Meaning that when we express the toxic hurt and fear that resides in our soul, we hurt ourselves.

And when we attempt to diminish the physiological sensations that we feel, we end up hurting ourselves.

Some internalized anger behaviors include drinking and drugging, infidelity, isolation, self-injury and the ultimate internalize anger behavior suicide.

Anger can also be turned on others or externalized. Often these behaviors hurt others more than hurting ourselves and include domestic or physical violence and assaults, verbal assault such as bullying, passive aggressive behaviors such as giving someone the cold soul shoulder and ultimately the externalized anger behavior of taking another's life.

So why should we heal anger?

Anger can be productive and unproductive.

Anger can be supportive and destructive.

Anger can be good and bad.

How do we know when our anger requires healing?

Depending on the outcome of your anger behavior you will decide whether you need healing.

If getting angry leads to a healthy and effective outcome then healing is not required.

On the other hand if you determine your anger behaviors lead to ineffective and unhealthy outcomes then you may choose to heal.

At the end of the day if you don't see your drinking and drugging as ineffective and unhealthy than there is nothing to heal.

On the other hand if you're drinking and drugging leads to missing work, becoming argumentative with friends, ignoring your family, cheating on your partner or being fired then perhaps you may see *those outcomes* as unhealthy and ineffective. If that's the case then you may want to get busy healing.

Anger can be a way in which some of us attempt to heal the trauma we experience as a result of the crises of our lives. Anger helps us eliminate the hurt and fear that is trapped in our soul.

Anger feels good.

Anger works.

However Anger can only feel good for short period of time. Anger usually becomes ineffective when we no longer get what we want. Anger becomes ineffective when we begin to create more broken attachments. Anger makes the crisis worst. Anger leads to more trauma.

Healing what hurts and managing what scares the tar out of us help us eliminate anger behaviors that create further destruction in our lives.

How Do You Heal Anger?

The problem with anger is that it can be productive. Anger can and does help us get what we need and want out of life.

Anger can also be a supportive behavior. When a coach gets thrown out of a game in support of his players because of poor officiating that anger behavior sends the message: "I support you! I stand behind you!"

However anger can also be very destructive. The same coach yelling at his players for their "stupid and dumb-ass play" does not send the message "I support you!" It sends the message "you suck".

Anger can be healing. In many ways anger behaviors can help us "right the wrongs" of our lives. When someone has wronged us and we in an assertive and self-advocating style communicate to that person who wounded us our pain and fear we are healing.

Anger is a behavior that has a large continuum of effect. Meaning it's not what you say but how you say it that we associate people to being angry. You can be in physical control of your body, using very specific language, managing all of your emotions and still be angry. Yet when you cross that line and you lose physical control of your body, you use language that is damaging and you no longer manage your emotions anger is simply the avoidance of healing and the emotional vomiting on another and leveraged to quickly get what it is that we want.

You can express your hurt and fear through anger behaviors in a responsible way or in an irresponsible way. At the end of the day it all depends on the outcome of your choice. The coach who chooses to argue with the officials because of poor officiating shows support for his team and goes the locker room proud of his/her accomplishment. On the other hand the coach who sits in his office after a game holding with his head in his hands ashamed of how he treated his/her players is also pondering the outcome of his/her behavioral choices.

Anger can be a means to heal trauma. Anger is incredibly efficient at helping us express the hurt and fear that plagues our souls. Anger is the quickest valve for the elimination of the toxic emotions that haunt the very depths of our being. As our hurt and fear is extracted from our souls through anger behaviors we feel good. The toxicity that brews within is lessened, in terms of volume, and the physiological sensations we experience are quieted. If only for a moment.

Anger becomes ineffective when we realize we are not going to get what we want to. When the outcome or the goal of our behaviors is not realized anger, like any other behavior is ineffective. When that ineffective behavior destroys relationships and connections we have with important and vital people places and things, anger becomes unhealthy.

Anger can initiate even more crisis in our life.

Anger can lead to even more trauma that we must triage.

Anger can be productive yet so unproductive. It is such a fine line.

In order to keep anger from becoming an ineffective and unhealthy behavioral choice we must first heal what actually fuels anger behaviors: hurt and fear. If hurt and fear are eliminated ineffective and unhealthy anger behaviors will no longer become a behavioral choice.

Some of the things that I have read and done when it comes to "anger management" are nothing more than delay tactics for healing. Why would you ever try to *"manage"* something you are trying to eliminate? Would you ever manage your alcoholic consumption if you are indeed addicted? Would you manage or infidelity and affairs if you are attempting to save your relationship? The goal is to eliminate ineffective and unhealthy anger behaviors by healing the hurt and fear that actually fuel the behavior we are attempting to eliminate.

When we know something, then we are aware. For example you may know that I am a counselor who holds a master of arts in counseling psychology and that I am a licensed clinical professional counselor in the state of Illinois. If you knew that prior to reading the last sentence than you were aware of some of my credentials. If you were unaware until a few moments ago now you are aware.

When we understand and are aware of what we know, we are insightful. Now that you are aware of my credentials you may have the insight that I am not only an individual who has experienced many crises in my life I am also formally trained as a counselor. This unique combination may fuel your insight leading to an understanding that I am worthy of reading and I know what I am talking about.

Awareness is a knowledge of facts. When you are driving you may be aware of the fact that there is a car waiting at the stoplight immediately to your right. Awareness is also the mindfulness of life events. You may be aware that when a car is at a stoplight immediately to your right that car may be operated by a driver who would very much like to pass you once the light turns green. You are aware of this and mindful because you have experienced this life event before. If you have never been passed on the right by an eager driver after the light has turned green than you are about to have a life experience that will generate awareness. Awareness is also mindfulness of the surroundings of your immediate focus. You may be aware and mindful of a merge of the two lanes in which you and the other driver occupied less than 1/4 mile past the stoplight.

As I have discussed earlier Dr. Albert Ellis is A-B-C model suggests that "**A**" is for "*action*". An action is something that occurs in your everyday life. It is the moments in life that collectively make up the experience of living. In short things happen. Our brains make a mental note of these life. We are aware of these facts and mindful of their importance in our lives.

In order for healing to take effect we must be aware of the facts that make up the things that happen in life. We must be aware of the people, places and things that impact our life each and every day. Failure to be aware and mindful of the connections that touch our lives each and every day simply will not allow healing to occur.

When we have insight, our minds interpret the facts that our brains collect. Our brains indicates to us that there is a car to our right as we wait at a stoplight. Our insight tells us that cars to our right often attempt to pass on the right just before the merge 1/4 mile past the stoplight. We are insightful of this behavior. Our brains have collected and stored this fact thanks to prior experience. Our insight is triggered when our brains present the familiar set of facts. We're also insightful of our surroundings including the fact that there is no way on God's green earth that we are going to allow the driver to pass in 1/4 mile. We are insightful because the brain tells us our blood pressure has just gone up a tick, are palms are now sweating, we're taking deeper breaths, there is a tingle down our spine. The brain is aware of all of our physiological responses to the surroundings and the facts that the brain has already collected. Our insights and imagination, as if working with a jigsaw puzzle, assembles the pieces into one coherent and clear picture for us which ultimately drives our behavioral choices. The things in which we are aware are the actions of our lives or the "A" of Albert Ellis is ABC model. When our mind and brain work together to formulate one clear and cohesive picture, we have triggered, created or recalled from the recesses of our mind a belief or B in Albert Ellis is ABC model. Our emotive and physiological responses to that belief that there is no way on god's green earth I am allowing that driver in that car to pass me on the right in the next quarter mile triggers what Albert Ellis refers to a C or consequences in his ABC model. The only element remaining is our behavioral choice. With the belief that there is no way on god's green earth I am allowing that driver in that car to pass me on the right in full bloom the behavioral consequence most likely to be automatically and deliberately selected is to put the pedal to the metal baby!

There will be an outcome to our spontaneous drag race: perhaps a crash, perhaps a couple of flying birds given to each driver, perhaps the driver to the right had no intention of passing an our speed is for naught or gets us a ticket from the police officer stationed an 8th of a mile past the stoplight. A police officer whom we do not see because we were so focused on the action surrounding us and the belief triggered as our mind and brain processed our surroundings.

With each and every event in our life there is always an evaluation period the outcome of our behaviors become the new action in the ABC model of Albert Ellis continues indefinitely as its cycles through our life.

With every evaluation of our consequence or the outcome of all or selected behaviors triggered by our beliefs we become aware of our own in other people's reactions to our behaviors. The awareness of their response leads to insight as to whether or not the behavior we selected was healthy or on healthy, ineffective or effective. Our beliefs may be altered or reinforced as a result of our evaluation of the consequences or outcomes that resulted from our behavior. If we are to accept any kind of personal responsibility for our own healing and mental wellness we must have the psychological fitness skills of awareness and insight. At the end of the day healing occurs when our insight is put into action.

If after putting the pedal to the metal the outcome is that I cause a wreck, for someone to drive on the shoulder, get a speeding ticket or simply feel like a horse's ass my insight may be that my sickening guilty feeling is not worth the 100 feet of asphalt that I gained over another individual. Not wanting to feel the toxic guilt or shame anymore I resolve as a means of my insight to no longer fight another driver. Rather I will take a gracious approach and allow that other driver time to merge if indeed they need to be, one to be calm I have to be in front of me.

Addiction: a Grieving Train Wreck

Before I begin this chapter let's get out a few presumptions out of the way:

1. A lot of people out there can actually manage their alcohol consumption.
2. Cocaine, heroin, meth and all of the street drugs are illegal.
3. There are many, many, many addictions.

An addiction is a coping technique or behavior that used to work well and is now ineffective and unhealthy. Nobody starts to consume alcohol, surf the Internet for porn, posts to Instagram, consumes a gallon of ice cream after a bad day for the sole purpose of initiating and supporting an addiction. Addictions grow over time. Addictions start out as an innocent attempt to manage then stress of life but eventually overwhelm and become ineffective and unhealthy.

Addictions are nothing more than behaviors that help us express and expel that hurt and fear that haunts our soul as the result of a crisis event. Addictions also help us calm the physiological sensations that occur when we think about and ponder a really bad day in our life. When I am unable to cope with the intense pain of losing a loved one I may turn to an addictive behavior that helps me express and expel that pain and at the same time quiets my body's response so that I am no longer consumed by that event.

As I said earlier there are many, many addictions. Some of the more common include drinking and drugging, Internet usage, food, television binging, computer gaming, isolation, church and volunteering and your career. Remember an addiction is any healing behavior that is simply become ineffective or unhealthy based on your evaluation. It's not an addiction until you have decided the behavior is no longer healthy and effective at helping you improve the quality of your life.

Addictions are selected behavior. We choose to engage in these activities in an effort to help us manage the stress of life and heal what wounds our soul. There are many steps I took to get drunk. There were many opportunities for me not to drive the car to the bar, to not park, to not get out of the car, to not go into the bar, to not sit down at the bar, to not order that beer, to not put that beer to my mouth and ultimately to not swallow the alcohol. At the end of the night when I was thanking a toilet for being cool and wet every step I took to that point was within my control. I had to accept that fact in order to alter my behaviors. My actions may have seemed automatic or that those choices and actions were out of my control…they aren't. My actions only become the norm over the course of me leveraging these behaviors overtime.

We justify the selected addictive behavior that we engage because they were once effective. Drinking alcohol at one point in my life eliminated social anxiety I experienced. Therefore I kept returning to something that initially offered me relief. Often we justify addictive, unhealthy and ineffective behaviors with logic. I don't drive when I drink. I only drink at home. Hey the "I have needs and my wife often has 'headache' so who cares if I surf the Internet for hours? What's wrong with playing video games all night? I'm on vacation! God wants me to volunteer every day at my church.

Addictions are triggered by how we think about our daily life. As I've stated before in this book Dr. Albert Ellis' Rational Emotive Behavioral Therapy uses the ABC model. "A" is for action. When things occur in our life, such as a tough day at work, we respond with the belief I a drink. Then suddenly it is Miller time and the consequences quickly follow. Albert Ellis' "A" is for action may be that my in law's are coming for a visit. The belief triggered is I need to find a way to relax so I'm not divorced. Where are my smokes? Becomes the consequence. Or perhaps when you arrive home after a stressful day you avoid your family and go to the "men gave" for little "me time".

Addictions are fueled by our automatic emotive responses to the stress of our life. When I am fearful, I drink in an effort to eliminate that anxiety. When I'm feeling wounded and hurt, I may turn to food to comfort me. Addictions are also fueled by the automatic physiological sensations we experience as a result of our mind interpreting the world around us. If I am afraid I may experience physical sensations that are quieted as a result of smoking a joint or snorting some cocaine.

Our addictions are learned coping techniques. We try something it works and we return to it time and time again. Like any behavior an addiction is strengthened the more we use it. The more we evaluate it as being effective and healthy the stronger it becomes and the more difficult it is to break that pattern. When we drink the anxiety goes away and that is a good thing so we continue to return to alcohol to manage anxiety. When I have a session with Ben and Jerry and need a gallon of ice cream my depression is lifted. I will schedule sessions with Ben and Jerry weekly even if I gain 1000 pounds. When I smoke I can socialize. When I do heroin I'm able to deal with my family.

Healing Addiction

I will never forget the day that a young, female intake specialist said to me, "we think you might have an addiction to alcohol and drugs."

REALLY?!

Think? Interesting word choice. Her soft eyes somewhat contradicted her hesitant tone that accompanied her diagnosis. Almost as if when was scared to tell me that I was an addict and drunk. We had just spent forty-five minutes or so together. She asked questions. I answered. Then, the cautious tale of the outcome of that assessment.

Can't say I was shocked.

Can't say I wasn't shocked.

I was sort of ambivalent to the whole thing. Sort of like when I had broken my foot. I walked on it for months thinking I had pulled a muscle. Once the pain became a little bit too much to handle and everyone in my life told me to go to the doctor's office, I did. And with that diagnosis, can't say I was or wasn't shocked.

It was what it was. A broken foot or a manner in which I dealt with me believing that my life, at the time of my addiction assessment, tasted like a cardboard dirt sandwich with a side of saw dust.

Alright. Life sucks and I deal with it by drinking, drugging and partying. What's wrong with that?

Nothing. My addition is my addiction. My issues were not my addictive behaviors as those worked as planned. I drank and felt comfortable in my own skin. I took drugs and I was able to escape. I had sex and could forget about my shitty life for a while and feel good doing it.

Nope. My addiction was doing exactly what it was supposed to do. Rejuvenate life.

The addiction was not the issue for me. Nope. The issue was the outcome generated as a result of engaging in my addiction behaviors.

Being arrested.

Getting fired.

Tossing my wife out of my life.

Ruining friendships.

Yep. These things created more problems for me and added to the already growing sense that my life sucked-ass. What I though was helping me deal with an ass-sucking life really just made matters worse the next day.

Something was not working.

My life, was "fun" while drinking, drugging and having lots of sex, yet when that short term fix ended, my life sucked once again. And I needed more and more "fun" to cover up the grown suck-ass life.

I chose healing. I chose recovery. Sobriety.

Again, choosing healing was the more difficult choice that staying the course. Recovery from an addiction is a scorched earth healing process. All must go. Friends, activities, hang-outs. It all has to go.

And it all went.

As I would any behavior that I have decided is no longer effective and healthy or should be a part of my psychological fitness skills that lead to our overall mental wellness…I eliminated my addiction behaviors. I changed the places I visited, the things I did and the people with whom I connected.

In short, I blew up my life.

I started over.

Those who have an addiction, a coping technique that at one time was considered healthy and effective then over time become unhealthy and ineffective need the following during their recovery:

- Acceptance
- Fellowship
- Hope and encouragement
- Anonymity
- A low level of obligation expected from membership
- Education and guidance from committed members of a sobriety or recovery team.

If you, like me, are attempting to eliminate an addictive behavior the first "thing" I and people in recovery need, and as 12-Step programs suggest in the first three steps, is a "surrendering" to or acceptance of the notion that the addiction, as an attempt to heal, is no longer working. In addition to surrendering one must also accept that the chosen healing behavior, a.k.a. an addiction, needs to be eliminated.

That's tough: accept that your favorite coping technique may need to be, maybe, kind of eliminated?

Are you kidding?

How am I supposed to cope?

This is the point where many people decided "no way am I going to give up the one thing that truly helps me cope with and deal with the *bullshit of life*, the stress of life!"

Can't do it.

Nope. No way possible.

Can't see doing *THAT*!

And at this point, I and others, still do not fully realize that letting go of the incredibly warm and needed security blanket of my/our addiction is the first of many losses on the road to sobriety.

I drove to my very first AA meeting post my intensive outpatient 28 day program. I parked in the lot outside of the church where the meeting gathered. I popped open the cooler I had in the trunk of car. I opened one of the ice cold beers I had stored in the cooler for such an event. Lite a smoke and tried to decide if I was ready to "go in."

One smoke did not offer enough deliberation time for me so I lite another and continued my internal deliberation.

I drove away.

The next day I tried again.

Then again the day after that.

Eventually I went in.

It sucked. I thought that my life, as I knew it was over.

The second "thing" I and people in recovery need, as 12-Step programs suggest in steps four through nine, is the development of personal responsibility for one's choices as well as accountability for the outcome of those choices. Fun, fun fun!

I chose to drink and drug.

I chose to drive drunk.

I chose to hurt people.

I chose to isolate and alienate.

Me. I did those things.

And I need to take responsibility for the choices I had made and the outcomes of those choices.

And finally, the third "thing" I and people in recovery need, as 12-Step programs suggest in steps, is a dedication to a spiritual awakening or a new sense of mental wellness.

At the end of the day, the *Art of Healing* from anger, addition and the storms of life require a sense of renewal, rejuvenation and a sense of purpose.

For me, this occurred when I accepted that I didn't need to be perfect. Healing is trial and error.

Appendix A: Real Damage in Real Life

On November 17, 2013, a natural wind/rain storm hit Illinois. For the first time in my life, the kind of debris and damage I have used in my workshops, seminars, addresses, books and radio shows for years actually occurred in my real life.

End Notes:

References used in the creation of the book.

[i] Glasser, William, MD, *Choice Theory: A New Psychology of Personal Freedom, HarperPerennial, 1998.*
[ii] Psychological Fitness Skills is a copy write held by Fat Guy in Spandex Media Productions, 2013